THE LIBRARY
ST. MARY'S COLLEGE OF MARYLAND
ST. MARY'S CITY, MARYLAND 20686

D1684743

Photo by Romulus Linney
David Van Pelt, Christopher Roberts, Rebecca Harris, Heather Melton, T. Cat Ford, and Christopher Cappiello in the Theater for the New City production of *Gint* at the 1998 Isben Festival, National Theatre of Norway, Oslo.

GINT

A Play in Two Acts
from Henrik Ibsen's PEER GYNT

BY
ROMULUS LINNEY

DRAMATISTS
PLAY SERVICE
INC.

GINT
Copyright © 1999, Romulus Linney
Copyright © 1996, Romulus Linney
as an unpublished dramatic composition

All Rights Reserved

CAUTION: Professionals and amateurs are hereby warned that performance of GINT is subject to a royalty. It is fully protected under the copyright laws of the United States of America, and of all countries covered by the International Copyright Union (including the Dominion of Canada and the rest of the British Commonwealth), and of all countries covered by the Pan-American Copyright Convention, the Universal Copyright Convention, the Berne Convention, and of all countries with which the United States has reciprocal copyright relations. All rights, including professional/amateur stage rights, motion picture, recitation, lecturing, public reading, radio broadcasting, television, video or sound recording, all other forms of mechanical or electronic reproduction, such as CD-ROM, CD-I, DVD, information storage and retrieval systems and photocopying, and the rights of translation into foreign languages, are strictly reserved. Particular emphasis is placed upon the matter of readings, permission for which must be secured from the Author's agent in writing.

The stage performance rights in GINT (other than first class rights) are controlled exclusively by the DRAMATISTS PLAY SERVICE, INC., 440 Park Avenue South, New York, N.Y. 10016. No professional or non-professional performance of the Play (excluding first class professional performance) may be given without obtaining in advance the written permission of the DRAMATISTS PLAY SERVICE, INC., and paying the requisite fee.

Inquiries concerning all other rights should be addressed to The Gersh Agency, 130 West 42nd Street, New York, NY 10036, Attn: Peter Hagan

SPECIAL NOTE

Anyone receiving permission to produce GINT is required to give credit to the Author as sole and exclusive Author of the Play on the title page of all programs distributed in connection with performances of the Play and in all instances in which the title of the Play appears for purposes of advertising, publicizing or otherwise exploiting the Play and/or a production thereof. The name of the Author must appear on a separate line, in which no other name appears, immediately beneath the title and in size of type equal to 50% of the largest, most prominent letter used for the title of the Play. No person, firm or entity may receive credit larger or more prominent than that accorded the Author.

For John Dillon

ACKNOWLEDGMENT

Professors Joan Templeton and Marvin Carlson, of the Ibsen Society of America, recommended the original production to Ellen Horn, Artistic Director of The National Theatre in Oslo, who brought it to Norway. The author thanks all three.

PEER GYNT is the Norwegian national epic, loved, revered and known almost by heart in Norway. This Appalachian version was accepted by its audiences, who understood its intent, that it respected Ibsen. And while it simplified a great many things, it never attempted to substitute anything.

I think these audiences were pleased that too much was not made of the Appalachian nature of the adaptation. They saw it was only a different way of presenting Ibsen's play. The set was bare wood. There were no folksy costumes, no Smoky Mountain music. All American folk aspects except the speech were sternly avoided. Ibsen was not trivialized.

Norwegian folklore, like Appalachian, is at its core stark and unvarnished. So the American folk language was used as a medium for inner personal reality, not local color. The bare platform and shifting lights focused on the emotional truth of PEER GYNT, not on its famous and dangerous theatrics, sometimes confusing. It was still the tale of a man who loses himself trying to find himself. Pete Gint's journey through his life remained Ibsen's, simple and solid, like a Norwegian or Appalachian landscape.

For the cast and the author, performing this play for the Ibsen Festival was an experience of lasting joy and satisfaction. We will always be grateful to The National Theatre and its audiences for a warm and knowing reception of GINT.

Romulus Linney

GINT opened at the Theater for the New City (Crystal Field, Producing Director) in New York on January 24, 1998. It was invited to the Ibsen Festival at The National Theatre in Oslo (Ellen Horn, Artistic Director) as the first American production of Ibsen to appear in Norway, and played there in September 1998. It was adapted from Henrik Ibsen's PEER GYNT. It was directed by Romulus Linney; the set design was by Mark Mercante; the costume design was by Jonathan Green; the lighting design was by Jon Andreadakis; the production manager was Anthony Pick; and the assistant directors were Robert Montgomery and Laura Callanan. The cast was as follows:

PETE GINT	David Van Pelt
OLDIE MOMMA	Christine Parks
SALLY VICKS	Susan Erickson*
OLDER MAN	Bill Cwikowski*
OLDER WOMAN	T. Cat Ford
MAN	Christopher Cappeillo
WOMAN	Heather Melton
YOUNGER MAN	Christopher Roberts
YOUNGER WOMAN	Rebecca Harris*

*At the Ibsen Festival, SALLY VICKS was played by Rebecca Harris, OLDER MAN by Scott Sowers and YOUNGER WOMAN by Adrienne Thompson.

GINT is freely adapted from the 1906 Richard Mansfield acting edition of PEER GYNT, translated by William and Charles Archer.

CHARACTERS
PETE GINT
OLDIE MOMMA
SALLY VICKS
SIX ACTORS PLAYING MANY PARTS
(See "Doubling"):
YOUNGER WOMAN
YOUNGER MAN
WOMAN
MAN
OLDER MAN
OLDER WOMAN

DOUBLING

OLDER MAN plays FATHER, HOG KING, BRESH, OLDER MAN AT OLDIE MOMMA'S DEATH, BILLIONAIRE, HEAD OF UNIVERSITY, PREACHER, MIST SPIRIT.

OLDER WOMAN plays MOTHER, HOG, BRESH, OLDER WOMAN AT OLDIE MOMMA'S DEATH, BILLIONAIRE, INMATE, VAGRANT, MIST SPIRIT.

MAN plays JONES, HOG, BRESH, MAN AT OLDIE MOMMA'S DEATH, BILLIONAIRE, INMATE, MEDICINE MAN, MIST SPIRIT.

WOMAN plays WEDDING GUEST 1, WOMAN, HOG, BRESH, BILLIONAIRE, DOCTOR THIGH, MIST SPIRIT.

YOUNGER MAN plays GROOM, HOG, BRESH, HOG-WOMAN'S SON, BILLIONAIRE, SCREWDRIVER INMATE, MIST SPIRIT.

YOUNGER WOMAN plays WEDDING GUEST 2, BRIDE, HOG, BRESH, YOUNGER WOMAN AT OLDIE MOMMA'S DEATH, BILLIONAIRE, GINT'S MISTRESS, INMATE, MIST SPIRIT.

TIME
1917 (ACT ONE)
1970 — 1997 (ACT TWO)

PLACE
The Appalachian mountains.

While each staging of GINT should be free and creative, these are the basic principles of its first production:

SETTING
The set for both New York and Oslo was a rectangular wooden platform two feet high, ramped on four sides. It was backed by a wooden wall. Two wooden crates, one large, one small, were used for a roof, benches, a coffin, etc. At opening, an old Appalachian quilt lay over one of the crates, at center, used later for the death of Oldie Momma.

COSTUMES
The costumes were plain black all purpose clothes, which were added to by a very few pieces. Gint was in a plain black T-shirt and ragged pants (no overalls, please) and in the second act wore a black shirt, black leather pants, and when very old, a raincoat. Others kept their costumes the same throughout.

PROPS
All the props of the play were mimed, with the exception of the two crates and the quilt, which were used for many purposes.

LIGHTING
The lighting was fluid and moved from place to place on the platform and the ramps. In the Bresh scene, many shadows. Special downlights of red for the end of the Hog scene and the Madhouse scene.

MUSIC
Familiar Appalachian music will trivialize the famous play. Early American music, unfamiliar to the general public, such as Shaker hymns and processionals, serve the purpose without overdoing it. In the original production, a quiet piece of Shaker music was used at the opening, the end of the first act, the beginning of the second, the end of the play and that was all.

GINT

ACT ONE

A wooden platform, ramped around on all four sides. The ramps are not steep but long, leading up to the center playing area. Behind this, sky, or a wall of wood, representing the mountain world.

Onstage are two sturdy wooden crates. One, about five feet by two feet, sits at the side of the stage. The other, smaller, three by two, is at center stage, covered by a colorful but ragged Appalachian strip quilt. All properties are mimed.

Nine actors walk up the ramps. They are young, and dressed very simply in back: women with long black wool skirts, men in black T-shirts and pants. They will all remain onstage throughout.

OLDER MAN
Gint, from Ibsen's *Peer Gynt*
OLDER WOMAN
The characters are, Pete Gint
(Actor playing Pete Gint raises his hand.)
YOUNGER MAN
His Oldie Momma
(Actress playing Oldie Momma raises her hand.)
YOUNGER WOMAN
Sally Vicks
(Actress playing Sally Vicks raises her hand.)

WOMAN
And six actors
(The six actors move to C.)
MAN
In Act One we play Pete Gint's neighbors
YOUNGER WOMAN
A bride
WOMAN
A slut
OLDER MAN
A coven of razorback hogs
YOUNGER MAN
A draft dodger
OLDER WOMAN
A talking forest
YOUNGER MAN
And a hog bastard son
OLDER MAN
The time in Act One is 1917
YOUNGER WOMAN
The place is the Appalachian Mountains of North Carolina
(The six actors and Sally Vicks move away. Oldie Momma sits on the crate, mad.)
OLDIE
It's a damn lie
(After her comes Pete Gint, 20 and handsome.)
GINT
Is not
OLDIE
No man in these mountains never did none of that
GINT
I did
OLDIE
Mortify yore lying self
sneaking around and sneaking around

not doing one lick of work nowhere

GINT
First that bear I come across
at Carson Falls

OLDIE
Six weeks with yore father's rifle-gun you lose
bringing back not one pound of nothing
but whiskey on yore breath

GINT
Then the stag
near Gillard's Creek

OLDIE
Look at you
pants and shirts ragtag messes
You expect me to believe yore fool stories
Ain't no bear near no Falls
ever soul knows they don't wash

GINT
This one did had a little cub with her
a-washing it
then she seen me
thought I was after her baby

OLDIE
Yes she would have

GINT
And you know what a black Momma bear'll
do to ary body she thinks'll harm her cub

OLDIE
I knowed more than one great hunter
met his end that way yes

GINT
So one second more and one of them paws'd
claw my head right off

OLDIE
Why didn't you shoot the beast
you had yore Daddy's gun

GINT
The damn thing misfired
bolt action blew up fell off
there I was
a raging black bear five foot away

OLDIE
Lord Jesus
no wait a minute
got me going again damn you
what then Pete
plunge a yard long barlow knife into the bear's throat
did ye conquer the dreadful beast did ye
Daniel Damned Hero Boone are ye

GINT
No Momma I ran

OLDIE
That I'll believe

GINT
That's how I come upon the magic stag

OLDIE
Aw God

GINT
I was a running down the rocks of the creekbed
so fast I couldn't stop myself
jest a jumping one t'other
way I did I was a boy you watching yelling
look out Pete
I was at my swimming hole
you know where that is

OLDIE
T'other side the creek
rocks are smooth and water's dark yes

GINT
So I jumped thisaway and a stag
jumped thataway
I plain landed on his back my hands
jest grabbed onto about four or five

generations of antlers he was old but fast
God Amighty like chain lightning
down Gillard's Creek we went

OLDIE
On the rocks
that ain't possible

GINT
I know it that's why I was so scared trying
think what to do get out my barlow knife
cut the things throat from its back
when yah he screamed

OLDIE
Screamed

GINT
Like I never heard no buck scream afore
flying through the air me on top
when yah
back snapped them antlers pinned me to him
and up Gillard's Creek we flew
and I said oh my Oldie Momma good-bye

OLDIE
Thought of me did ye

GINT
On the back of the demon stag I did
flying up the rocks

OLDIE
Wait a damn minute what about the falls
if you went back up what about the falls

GINT
Jumped the hell over them
We're flying over country above timberline
tops of balsam and pine beneath us
a high ridge in timothy grass I never seen afore

OLDIE
Timothy grass does grow timberline yes

GINT
A sqwaking bald eagle right by us flew
wings wide as this
and that'll scare to death even yore magic stag
and he fell

OLDIE
And you on his back

GINT
But Momma there's a shining lake up there
wherever we was and into that we fell

OLDIE
Into lake water yes

GINT
Splash stag and me swimming me holding on
he couldn't gore me swimming

OLDIE
Gore you oh no

GINT
So I let go swam
the absolute other way

OLDIE
Praise God

GINT
Come up on shore and ran
and ran and ran home to you

OLDIE
And you not hurt
praise God

GINT
And at's why the rifle-gun's gone
my clothes all a mess
but also why I'm alive

OLDIE
Oh son oh my boy

GINT
Living still

to love my Oldie Momma

OLDIE

Blessed angel baby
(Oldie Momma beats Gint with the quilt.)
God damned dog's hind leg
crooked lying
miserable mother's misery
What did I do to deserve a liar for a son
(Gint rolls at her feet, then jumps up, grabs her and tickles her.)

GINT

Hey Momma hey Momma

OLDIE

Pete stop stop that
(She laughs hard in spite of herself. They collapse on the crate together. He puts his head in her lap.)

GINT

Oldie Momma what do we care
I'm happy with you
Be happy with me

OLDIE

Happy I was happy
when yore Daddy was alive
me first married then I was happy
but now
farmhouse windows stopped with cardboard
old horse and carriage seat for furniture
fences all down
and a son telling lies
when he's been gone six weeks drinking and fighting
Heared you and Smithy Jones
squabbling over some girl
and you broke his arm

GINT

I did did I

OLDIE

Neighbors heared him yelling

GINT
No they didn't
they just told you that
'cause it was me yelling

OLDIE
You

GINT
Smithy Jones is powerful stout
and he give me the licking not t'other way round
I'll confess it

OLDIE
Then I spit
fight if you must being a man
but at least for Christ's sake win
did he hurt you

GINT
Hush Oldie Momma hush
what difference does it make
all these mountains will know my Momma
because she bore a man does something

OLDIE
But whut

GINT
Something great grand and glorious

OLDIE
Who you

GINT
Why not me
I can be anything I want to be

OLDIE
You could
but what do you do
Hillbrook's daughter fancied you
He's rich and you could of had her

GINT
I hink so

OLDIE
She wanted you any fool saw that
GINT
Hester Hillbrook
is wall-eyed spindly legged
and near thirty year old
I low rate any woman the day after
she hits sixteen
OLDIE
What does that matter the girl has land
and a house that's coming to her
Lord Jesus
GINT
I might have her at that
OLDIE
Not now you won't
GINT
Why not now
OLDIE
Whilst you were off six weeks riding some stag
Hester Hillbrook said yes to Thornton Stobbs
GINT
That fool
when's the wedding
OLDIE
Today wedding's to God damned day
what do you think I'm so mad about
GINT
Then we'll go
stop the fool thing
OLDIE
Shame me and you both
never
GINT
Then I'll do it myself

OLDIE
You will not
you leave them people be
GINT
Hester Hillbrook here's Pete Gint
giving you yore last chance
OLDIE
No never I'll go
tell ever soul you don't mean it
GINT
You can't get there from here
it's too far for you to walk
we sold the horse
OLDIE
I'm mad enough to climb fifty mountains
I'll plain tell the world
what a son I got
GINT
Not from the roof of the springhouse you won't
(Gint sets the larger crate on its end to one side and swings Oldie Momma up on it.)

OLDIE
What are you doing to me
son get me down from here
GINT
Play like you're on at stag's back
and I'll take care of the rest
OLDIE
Pete Pete you come back here
(Gint runs away, then dashes back to the center of the platform.)
GINT
There's the house everybody's there
Best fergit this go back home
God I wish I had a drink
(Enter Woman and Younger Woman.)

WOMAN
Father a drunk
YOUNGER WOMAN
Mother fifty year old the day he was born
WOMAN
Too close
YOUNGER WOMAN
Crazy son
WOMAN
Crazy momma
WOMAN AND YOUNGER WOMAN
Too close
(They pass on to the wedding.)

GINT
Me and my Momma they were talking about
my Momma never done them no harm
why they so mean to us
well sticks and stones hell with them
(Gint flops down on the platform, on his back, arms outspread. Sunlight through clouds passes over him.)
Beautiful day in the mountains
look at that cloud yonder like a horse
with a man on it
and yah
Pete Gint rides alone
on a white horse with golden horseshoes
dressed in spotless linen suit
oh he's good looking
people waving hats at him
cheering him on
to his great destiny
Kings take off their crowns and they say
(He starts to get up. Enter Man, putting a foot on his chest.)
MAN
Look who's here
GINT
Huh

Oh Jones
MAN
Where you been Pete
six weeks now since I give you a licking
and I'm waiting to give you anothern
GINT
Never mind where I been
and next time it's you'll be knocked down
MAN
Of a sartin
Going to Hester's wedding
GINT
None of yore business where I'm going
MAN
She was hot for you onct ain't it so
GINT
Shut up about that
MAN
She jilted you flat but
come on to the dance
should be an old widow or wall flower
left there for you
So long

(Exit Man.)

GINT
I'll kill him
Next time I'll kill the bastard
wait a minute
britches torn rags dirt
I'm a sight
If I had a white linen suit now
be different
But I don't
damn
who them girls just getting there
five or six for ever man easy pickings
and the fiddlers coming

to hell with everthing
I'm jumpin' in
(Gint runs off the platform, as on behind him come Older Man and Younger Man.)

YOUNGER MAN
Daddy
she's locked herself in the bedroom
she won't let me in

OLDER MAN
Knock down the door

YOUNGER MAN
She won't let me

OLDER MAN
You can't get it
you don't deserve it

YOUNGER MAN
Daddy

OLDER MAN
Don't Daddy me
be a man
for Christ's sake

(Exit Older Man and Younger Man. Enter Younger Woman, Woman, and Man.)

YOUNGER WOMAN
I want to dance

WOMAN
So do I

MAN
Come on then

YOUNGER WOMAN
Hold it
Look who's here

(Enter Gint.)

GINT
Who wants to dance
you

YOUNGER WOMAN
No sir

GINT
You then

WOMAN
No sir

GINT
Any soul at all

MAN
Don't look like it do it

(Exit Man, Woman, Younger Woman.)

GINT
Nasty looks and burning whispers
mean smiles God they hurt a man

(Enter Sally Vicks.)

Who are you

SALLY VICKS
Sally Vicks
we just moved to this valley

GINT
Who's we

SALLY VICKS
Mother father little sister and me

GINT
No husband

SALLY VICKS
No sir

GINT
You want to dance

SALLY VICKS
Yes sir after I pay my respects
to my hosts excuse me

(Exit Sally Vicks.)

GINT
Now who's that

I mean good looking piece
plain open honest looking
and that body under that dress I mean
what kind of girl is that
(Enter Woman, Man and Younger Woman.)

WOMAN
Hey Pete
Good straight whiskey going around

YOUNGER WOMAN
We know how you fancy it

MAN
Have some

WOMAN
Wake us all up

GINT
Get that likker away from me
I ain't getting drunk now

WOMAN
Why not

YOUNGER WOMAN
You're a sight more fun when you do

(Exit Man, Woman, Younger Woman.)

GINT
I want to dance now
with that nice girl
where'd she go

(Enter Sally Vicks.)

SALLY VICKS
Are you the gentleman wanted to dance

GINT
I am

SALLY VICKS
What's yore name

GINT
Pete Gint

SALLY VICKS
Oh
oh Pete Gint oh
I'm sorry I forgot something
(Sally Vicks runs away.)
GINT
Forgot what
Well damn
(Enter Younger Man, Older Man and Older Woman.)
GROOM
Mother she just won't let me
OLDER WOMAN
Let you what
OLDER MAN
What do you think
YOUNGER MAN
She won't unlock the door
OLDER MAN
Ain't fit to kiss a dog
OLDER WOMAN
Give him time
you had yore own trouble
our wedding night
remember
OLDER MAN
Woman shut up
(Exit Older Man, Older Woman, Younger Man. Enter Woman, Younger Woman, Man.)
WOMAN
Come on Pete drink up
YOUNGER WOMAN
Everybody else is
GINT
Well hell gimmee
gimmee
(Woman mimes handing Gint a bottle and he mimes drinking th

whole bottle at once.)

          WOMAN
          Let's see it Pete
          MAN
          Drink up Pete
          YOUNGER WOMAN
          Guzzle it down
          MAN
          'Til you can't walk
          WOMAN
          Or talk
          YOUNGER WOMAN
          Just stink like a still
          ALL
          Yah

(Gint mimes draining the bottle and throwing it back at them. Man catches it. They laugh and exit. Gint, on his hands and knees, is drunk. Enter Sally Vicks. He gets up.)

          SALLY VICKS
          I shouldn't have done that
          GINT
          Done what
          SALLY VICKS
          Gone off on you like that
          I was just scared not no more
          GINT
          Well you're back now let's dance
          SALLY VICKS
          All right

(Sally Vicks pulls away.)

          You've been drinking
          I smell it on yore breath
          GINT
          What if I have

SALLY VICKS
You're wild

GINT
So's a healthy stag
when spring comes and life calls
now I'm calling you

SALLY VICKS
And you think I'll answer
just like that

GINT
Real women have been known to

SALLY VICKS
Yore kind of a real woman
and mine are something else

GINT
Be my kind tonight
and yores tomorrow

SALLY VICKS
Don't talk to me like that
I won't have it

GINT
You're ashamed what I look like

SALLY VICKS
No

GINT
I look like a tramp

SALLY VICKS
Not to me

GINT
Get drunk yes
but that was to spite you
mocking me just like everbody else
when all I aimed to do was please you

SALLY VICKS
Stop it

GINT
Stop what
you think you can tell me what to do
I can do all sorts of things
turn myself into a mountain lion
come to yore sweet bed at night
snorting and scrumping
don't think it's the cat
it's me Pete Gint
drink yore blood eat yore skin
and like a hog
suck you all over

SALLY VICKS
Now you're acting ugly

GINT
Arms and legs and neck and throat
legs belly and tits

SALLY VICKS
Good-bye

GINT
Stop wait
just dance with me

SALLY VICKS
How can I now

(Exit Sally Vicks. Enter Younger Man. Oldie Momma gets herself down from the crate.)

YOUNGER MAN
Pete you can help me
I got to get to my wife
she's locked herself in the bedroom
and won't come out

GINT
Ain't studying yore wife

GROOM
I'll pay you man
besides look
that Sally Vicks is leaving

GINT
Yeah without a word
no good-bye nothing
so where is the blushing damn bride

GROOM
In the bedroom

GINT
Bedroom is it
come on then

(Exit Gint and Younger Man. Enter Man, drunk, with Woman.)

MAN
Where is he that damned Gint

WOMAN
Give it to him Smithy

YOUNGER WOMAN
Thinking his little Miss Priss
so much bettern us

WOMAN
Fix him good

YOUNGER WOMAN
Beat the hell out of him

(Enter Oldie Momma.)

OLDIE
Where's Pete

YOUNGER WOMAN
Don't get excited Oldie Momma

WOMAN
Let Jones do it

OLDIE
Do what

MAN
Bust yore fool son's neck

OLDIE
Try to hurt my Pete
you'll answer to me

(Enter Groom. Exit Younger Woman.)

     GROOM
    Mother Father
     FATHER
     What

     GROOM
    Pete Gint

     OLDIE
   Is he all right

     GROOM
   He's got my wife
   look up there
   on the ridge

(He points. In a group, they all look up.)

     WOMAN
   He's got Hester
   He's stole the bride

    YOUNGER MAN
   Right out of the bedroom

     OLDIE
   Oh Pete

     WOMAN
  Got her over his shoulder

     MAN
   Like a sack of potatoes

    YOUNGER MAN
   He's stealing my wife

     WOMAN
   Get the law

    OLDER MAN
   Track him down

     MAN
   Throw him in jail

     WOMAN
   Look at him go

OLDIE
I wish he'd fall and break his neck

(All gasp.)

careful son be careful

(All exit, revealing Gint and Younger Woman, sitting behind them. Younger Woman tries to caress Gint.)

GINT
Stay away from me

YOUNGER WOMAN
After what we done how can I
you stole me from my husband
had yore way with me
man and wife eyes of God
and that's different

GINT
Why different you go yore way I go mine
hell with all wimmen
but one

YOUNGER WOMAN
And who's that

GINT
It ain't you

YOUNGER WOMAN
Who then bettern me

GINT
You look a man in the eye cheerful but modest
you allow no fooling
and make a man feel respect
do you hell no

YOUNGER WOMAN
No that ain't me

GINT
Do you come back to the dance
even when scared
tell a man he's wild
but stand by him best you can

YOUNGER WOMAN
Listen Pete

GINT
Are you honest and shy
when I talk randy foolishness
do you say stop and mean it

YOUNGER WOMAN
You're crazy

GINT
Do you make me feel
I'm a good man

YOUNGER WOMAN
No because you're not

GINT
Then what does it matter good-bye

YOUNGER WOMAN
Keep me keep my farm
everthing I have

GINT
Can't do it
man with a future like mine
can't afford no snakey woman like you

YOUNGER WOMAN
You'll wish you had
when you're dirt poor
and the law after you

(Younger Woman starts away.)

GINT
Enough of this disputation
All wimmen are the damn devil

YOUNGER WOMAN
All but one

GINT
All but one yes all but one

(Exit Younger Woman. Exit Gint. Lights darken and flash. Enter Oldie Momma and Sally Vicks, holding up the quilt. They sit,

huddled together in a rainstorm.)

OLDIE
Sky thunder wind storm and rain
keeping me from my boy
oh God
is that him Pete
up there coming through the pass
there

SALLY VICKS
No Oldie Gint it's not

OLDIE
Nothing nowhere
My boy lost

SALLY VICKS
Lost is the word all right

OLDIE
No not so
he's smart as a whip
but when a shiftless daddy walks out
you either drink and beat the child
or do what we did tell stories together
he'd be a Cherokee Indian me a Queen going to a castle
how'd I know they'd lead to wildness drinking
bears in waterfalls
and riding stags in the air

SALLY VICKS
Hush we just have to wait
while they look for him

OLDIE
I reckon
much obliged you helping an old woman

SALLY VICKS
While we wait
tell me more

OLDIE
Tell you what

SALLY VICKS
Everything about him
OLDIE
You'll tire of listening
fore I'll ever tire of talking
SALLY VICKS
Everything please
OLDIE
Well
I was fifty year and one month
when he was borned
that was in June hot and sticky it was
(Exit Oldie Momma and Sally Vicks. Enter Gint. Storm lights flash.)

GINT
All after me
guns by God sticks and stones
But I outrun 'em
I'm young I'm strong
Oh hell yes
this is life
to beat the storm
me just as hard
me just as powerful
as ary thing there is
everthing else is a lie

(Lights brighten.)

What's this storm's over
rainbow
lights makes everthing clear
I see my life too
it hurts what I done
stealing that stupid woman
having her in the dirt God
forget it

(Gint looks up.)

yonder two ravens sailing on the updrafts

      well I'll fly like that
I'll wash myself clean in a mountain stream
  and do great things in spite of them all
      and I'll be a great man
(Enter Woman, walking past Gint. He follows her.)

GINT
Now don't run off

WOMAN
But do you mean it

GINT
Of a certain
damn you're a piece

WOMAN
Think so do you

GINT
Purely do
take good care of you

WOMAN
Never hit me
like men do to women

GINT
Not me I'm the son
of gentlemen in these mountains

WOMAN
Son of gentlemen are you

GINT
I might be

WOMAN
My father's no gentleman
he's a king

GINT
Hush
no kings on these mountains

WOMAN
There are inside them

GINT
Inside

WOMAN
In caverns deep inside
my father rules

GINT
My mother's farm is bigger than caverns

WOMAN
My father is King Biggie

GINT
My mother is Queen Oldie

WOMAN
When my father gets mad
rocks split open

GINT
When my Momma yells they bounce

WOMAN
Do you wear any clothes
besides them rags

GINT
My Sunday suit it's white linen
this is everday

WOMAN
My everday dress
is gold and silk

GINT
If you're wearing it now
looks to me like mud and hay

WOMAN
Black can seem white
ugly beautiful
can it

GINT
Well big can seem little
dirty clean

WOMAN
And cat looks big till dog shows up
kiss me dog
(They kiss, greedily, stare at each other.)

GINT
How's that

WOMAN
You're the man for me we fit

GINT
Like legs in pants
like hands in gloves

(The Woman calls out.)

WOMAN
Hey you there
by my father's power
come here to us
and carry us to him

(Man, Younger Man, Younger Woman, and Older Woman turn the large crate around and kneel at its corners. The Woman gets on top of it on her hands and knees and all look up, grinning.)

GINT
It's a razorback hog

WOMAN
Biggest you'll ever see get on

(Gint straddles the back of the Woman on the razorback hog. There are rope reins he grabs.)

I was so lonely I was so sad
and look here you are
nobody knows what life will bring

(The razorback hogs hit the floor in the rhythm of a running animal. Light increases on Gint, riding his beast.)

GINT
Yee-haw
Great men are known
by the what they ride

(Enter Older Man).

OLDER MAN
So
(The hog splits apart, becomes Razorback Hog Subjects. They are really mean, and believably so. Gint is on the floor in front of the Older Man, who sits on the box now, with his Hogs behind him. Woman sits to one side and watches.)

MAN
Eat the son of a bitch

OLDER WOMAN
He's been ramptious with the Hog's daughter

YOUNGER WOMAN
Pruney rolicky horny ramptious eat him

YOUNGER MAN
I'll eat his hands

MAN
I'll eat his head

YOUNGER WOMAN
I'll eat his pecker

OLDER WOMAN
I'll eat his balls

OLDER MAN
Hush up chilluns
young man don't have no razorback
or skinny hog legs like we're plagued with
want my daughter that it

GINT
And yore kingdom as her dowry

OLDER MAN
Don't want much does he
how about half whilst I'm a breathing
other half when I die

GINT
Done

OLDER MAN
But not so fast first

there's a whole passle of maybes
One
HOGS
GOOD CITIZENSHIP
OLDER MAN
Swear you never leave this mountain
or think about ary thing outside it
GINT
I'll consider that
OLDER MAN
Two
HOGS
COMMON SENSE
OLDER MAN
Let's see how smart you are
OLDER WOMAN
A riddle
YOUNGER WOMAN
See if he can figger it
MAN
If he can't let me at him
OLDER MAN
Answer me this
What is the difference betwixt hogs and men
GINT
Ain't none
since if he gets the chance
a hog'll eat a man
and a man will shore as hell
always eat a hog
OLDER MAN
At's exactly so
we're just alike except for this
out yonder under the shining sky of day
wise men say be yoreself
whilst here among razorback hogs we say

HOGS
Be nobody else but yoreself
OLDER MAN
There's a flintsharp difference here
do you see it
HOGS
Do you
GINT
Be yoreself
or be nobody else but yoreself
at's a little misty
but who cares yes I say yes
OLDER MAN
Three
HOGS
DOWN HOME LIVING
OLDER MAN
bring him some vittels here
(A mimed bowl is served up by a Hog.)
Hogs eat the pieces of cows and bulls
and all other kinds of innards
mixed up in mead soup
so drink that
GINT
Phew what a stink
HOGS
Said so said so
kill the son of a bitch
OLDER MAN
Afore you throw that away in pure disgust
at bowl is pure gold
and comes with my daughter
what about that
GINT
Oh
well a man has to change

maybe it ain't so putrid after all
and I'll get used to it
(Gint mimes drinking down the contents of the golden bowl. Horrible face. Older Man nods. Hogs applaud.)

OLDER MAN
Four

HOGS
RIGHT RELIGION

GINT
Huh

OLDER MAN
No Jesus here or nobody else neither
can't abide it
church bells split our brains
you worship you
just you being nobody but yoreself
yore good animal self
where's yore tail

GINT
My what

OLDER MAN
Get him a tail

(He pushes Gint onto the box.)

GINT
Ain't studying no hog's tail
get away from here

OLDER MAN
I said get him a tail

(Hogs mime getting a tail.)
Slap it on him
(Hogs slap a hog's tail on Gint's butt.)
Switch it around
see how you like it
(Gint switches his butt around. Hogs approve. Again. Hogs applaud. Again. Hogs cheer.)

GINT
Well it is said a man's no more than
a piece of sand or a beast in the field
I'd rather be a beast
I'll endure it what now

OLDER MAN
Five

HOGS
MARRIED LIFE

OLDER MAN
Now you get to see my daughter
for herself
I mean as she is
not some piece but my very own
daughter come forth

(Woman crawls forward, hair in her face, facing Gint. Gint shrinks back in horror.)

GINT
That ain't her
that's something entirely awful else
some scrawny ugly
milk sick cow-hog
what the hell

MAN
I said eat him

YOUNGER WOMAN
Cook him

OLDER WOMAN
Chew him

YOUNGER WOMAN
This is insulting

OLDER MAN
Want my kingdom
love my daughter

GINT
I was just joking

I still love you
beautiful darling
(Gint kisses her, with difficulty. She crawls away.)

OLDER MAN
And six

HOGS
NEW SIGHT

OLDER MAN
Human nature sees things all wrong
I got to rid you of that
forever

GINT
What you fixing to do now

OLDER MAN
Just a scratch
with one fingernail
across yore eyeball
so you'll see life as we do
yore bride will be beautiful
no more dancing cows and harps
but a loving honeywife
all pruney rolicky and horny

GINT
You're talking crazy now

OLDER MAN
But I'm not crazy
it's you are crazy
and me to fix that
with two scratches of two eyeballs

GINT
Will I ever see like a man again

OLDER MAN
Of course not never

GINT
I'm gone
(Gint jumps up but is seized by the Hogs, forced down on the box.)

OLDER MAN
It's easier to get in here than get out
you've got the makings of a great hog
why throw it away

(Gint fights them off.)

GINT
I don't mind drinking guts
don't mind a tail
don't even mind a cow for a wife if she's rich
but to never be able to change
go back to my real life
I'll never bargain on that
no sir

OLDER MAN
You ruined my daughter
you got to marry her

WOMAN
I'm pregnant see

GINT
That was fast

OLDER MAN
Come on now give me them eyeballs
to scratch

GINT
To hell with you
I won't do it

OLDER MAN
Always like this with human beings
sticking it to any woman you please
then run away
grow up give me them eyeballs

WOMAN
And be a daddy here

GINT
Get out of my way

OLDER MAN
Eat him
(All the Hogs attack Gint, who fights back.)

MAN
Eat his arms

YOUNGER WOMAN
Eat his legs

OLDER WOMAN
Eat his eyes

HOGS
Eat him eat him eat him
(The Hogs knock Gint down, pile on him, and bury their hog heads into his body, chewing on him.)

GINT
Oldie Momma help me
(Sally Vicks and Oldie Momma sing a doxology.)

SALLY VICKS AND OLDIE MOMMA
(Singing.)
PRAISE GOD FROM WHOM ALL BLESSING FLOW
PRAISE HIM ALL CREATURES HERE BELOW

HOGS
Ahhhh!

OLDER MAN
The church on the mountain

MAN HOG
They're singing hymns for him

OLDER WOMAN HOG
Splits our ears

OLDER MAN
Get deeper in the mountain

HOGS
Ahhhh!!!!

(Hogs run off, leaving Gint alone in a single light on the stage.)

SALLY VICKS AND OLDIE MOMMA
(Singing.)
>PRAISE HIM ABOVE YE HEAVENLY HOSTS
>PRAISE FATHER SON AND HOLY GHOST

(Lights change, become spectral. All move to edge of the platform and sit on it in a line, facing Gint.)

ALL
(Harsh unison whisper.)
>Pete Gint

GINT
>That's me who are you

ALL
>I am the Breshssss

GINT
>Well whoever you are so long

(Gint moves a step forward, stops. He is in a forest.)
>You get out of my way you hear

ALL
>Get around us Pete Gint
>The Breshsss says get around everthing

GINT
>What does that mean
>who are you

ALL
>I am the invisible forest inside the woods
>I am the Breshsss I am the thicket
>I am get out of trouble
>and I am the spirit of get around it

MAN
>Never mind what is

WOMAN
>Say it ain't

YOUNGER MAN
>Say it's something else

OLDER MAN
>And get around it

GINT
Why are you messing with me
ALL
I am telling you always go around
GINT
I maybe will and maybe won't
depends on how I feel
then I decide
(Gint puts out his hands, pushes at the forest.)
God how much of you is there

ALL
Fight Pete go ahead fight
try to clear me you can't
I am everywhere too thick for you
GINT
Can't get through here
can't get through there
all briars and mountain brush
thick as a wall
ALL
Go around Pete Gint
Get around Breshsss or perish
GINT
Never
ALL
Then I'll just let you die here
And leave you for buzzards
(Sally Vicks and Oldie Momma sing a doxology again.)
SALLY VICKS AND OLDIE MOMMA
(Singing.)
PRAISE GOD FROM WHOM ALL BLESSING FLOW
PRAISE HIM ALL CREATURES HERE BELOW
ALL
Ah hymns
that cuts me down
you are strong Gint

there are women behind you
dammit

(Exit all.)

good-bye
but remember

SALLY VICKS AND OLDIE MOMMA

(Singing.)

PRAISE HIM ABOVE YE HEAVENLY HOSTS
PRAISE FATHER SON AND HOLY GHOST

ALL

Go around

go around

(Change of light. Gint gets up, brushes himself off. Enter Sally Vicks.)

GINT

Sally Vicks

SALLY VICKS

Yes Pete it's me

GINT

Still scared of me

SALLY VICKS

A little not much

GINT

Scared I'll jump up and grab you
kiss you all over and hump and squeeze
and you know what

SALLY VICKS

Don't play the randy fool with me
there's more to it than that
so stop

GINT

Fool huh
Mountain Hog daughter all over me
one day the next fighting some shapeless forest
then you

SALLY VICKS
Still drinking

(Exit Sally Vicks.)

GINT
No come back
wait
well don't forget me
(Change of light. Gint goes to the larger box, turns it up on end.)
Whew
shew hard work
no Oldie Momma now to help me
feed me and make me wool shirts
got to cut my own wood
and build my own house
yes sir
wait a minute somebody coming
(He scrambles back of the box, looks over it. Enter Younger Man.)
What's this some man
no just a boy
(Younger Man looks all around. He kneels, mimes pulling something from his belt. He holds out and looks at it.)
A meat axe
What the hell is he doing with it
(The Younger Man puts his right hand down on the ground and holds the meat axe up in the air.)
Well what now
(Suddenly, with a scream, which All join, the Younger Man mimes cutting off his right hand. He staggers off quickly.)
He's chopped his hand off
My God
(Gint goes to the hand, mimes picking it up.)
Damn drastic thing to do
why I mean you can't replace it
his right hand too
God
(Gint throws the imaginary hand away.)
I couldn't do it
Think about such things maybe

      but do them
        never
      what for

(Enter Sally Vicks.)

SALLY VICKS
You said come back
well I have
what are you doing

GINT
Building a cabin
playing like it was a castle
it'll just be a hut in the woods

SALLY VICKS
I would share it with you
You said you wanted me

GINT
You was scared to come near me

SALLY VICKS
I was but not no more

GINT
Yore momma and yore poppa

SALLY VICKS
And my little sister
but as I listened and listened
to yore Oldie Momma
and when I saw you again
here in the wild forest
I couldn't sleep
my days were heavy and hard
nights full of dreams about you
so I left them all
here I am

GINT
You come to me

(Gint and Sally Vicks take each other's hands and look at each other.)

SALLY VICKS
You alone and nobody never else
God forgive me how I love you
I don't know how I don't know why
Love for Pete Gint I'll never comprehend
But it is here and here it will stay

GINT
And me how I love you
but you know I'm an outlaw
all my goods my farm my heritage
they'll take everything now

SALLY VICKS
Do you think for a farm
I left my family
it was for you

GINT
Then that's what I'll be
I'll be yore family

(Gint backs away, staring at her.)
Let me just look at you God
you are everything that's light and clear and good
I'll never get tired carrying you
I'll never hurt you or disgrace you
or treat you badly
I'll tear down this hut
and build you something better

SALLY VICKS
Whatever it is
will be home
the wind up here is fresh air
and I can breathe
there was no air below
the people use it all up
but here with the firs sighing above me
here I will stay

GINT
Are you sure

for always and always
SALLY VICKS
Done
I'll never leave you
GINT
Done
go in what we have then
I'll get roots for the fire
warm up what's there comfort yoreself
I'll be right back

(Sally Vicks goes behind the box.)

My girl's bettern any of em
found her I'll hold her for life
now my palace shall rise
my beautiful house

(Enter Younger Man. He takes the smaller box and sets it down in front of Gint and the larger box. He stares up at Gint. Enter Woman. Gint stares at the Younger Man.)

WOMAN
Hidy Gint
whilst you build yore house
ours will rise up right beside it

GINT
Who are you

WOMAN
Neighbors now
neighbors forever

GINT
I never seen you before in all my life

WOMAN
Shore you have
give yore daddy something good
he'll need it

(Younger Man mimes holding out a bottle.)

CHILD
Here Daddy
have a drink

GINT
Daddy Daddy
this thing is mine
WOMAN
Like he was made quick
he growed quick
just try to get out of it
GINT
So it's you is it
the Hog's daughter
fathering something on me
comes out of hogs
not men
I'll never believe this is mine
WOMAN
Hogs grow quick
looks like you
acts like you
deny you stuck it to me you can't
'cause he's the proof
so just throw that sweet talk woman out of yore hut
and let yore real family
move in
(The Woman and the Younger Man press up against Gint.)
GINT
Get out of here hogwoman
WOMAN
God damn lover
I ain't afraid of you
I'll come see you ever single day
of ever single year
set yore door ajar and watch you both
when you're all sweet
and loving
you and yore goody goody Sally Vicks
go on kiss her

and hug her close and when you do
there I'll be laughing
sitting right there taking my turn
what can she say when she sees me
I got yore brat don't I
yore spiting image
honey hug yore father
(The Younger Man puts his arms around Gint's waist.)
YOUNGER MAN
I'll hug him all right
and when I grow up
I'll break his *back* for him
GINT
Sally Vicks
my innocent Sally Vicks
WOMAN
Poor Sally Vicks
well the Devil says it this way
when his father got drunk
he hit his mother
and she hit him
and that's how we all get hurt
we'll be right here Gint
YOUNGER MAN
Daddy
(Exit Woman and Younger Man. Gint stares after them.)
GINT
Dirt and disgrace
steal a man's wife for one night
then a hog slut mistress
with a hog bastard son
devil take women
that damn Bresh knowed what he was talking about
go around he said
my beautiful home smash
and a wall around Sally Vicks I can't jump
so roundabout Gint

for there is no way through this nastiness
I can't do this to her
(Sally Vicks calls for him.)

SALLY VICKS
Pete are you coming

GINT
Go around

SALLY VICKS
What

GINT
You got to wait Sally
it's dark and there's something I have to find

SALLY VICKS
Let me help you
whatever it is we'll both do it

GINT
No not this we can't
stay where you are
I'll do it alone

SALLY VICKS
All right Pete
don't go off too far

GINT
Be patient honey
I'll be awhile
you just wait

SALLY VICKS
I will
I'll wait

(Exit Sally Vicks on one ramp, Gint another. Enter Man, Younger Woman, Older Man and Older Woman. They move the large crate to center, and drape the quilt over it.)

OLDER WOMAN
They didn't have to take everthing away
(Oldie Momma enters and sits on the crate like it is a bed. She pulls the quilt over her legs.)

YOUNGER WOMAN
Left her a child's bed some rope
and a box of junk
pert near all

OLDER MAN
All because of that boy of hers

OLDIE
Don't say nothing
agin my boy
I'll be all right
when he gets home

OLDER WOMAN
If he gets home

OLDER MAN
You should have thrown him out years ago

MAN
Let him grow up and find his own way

OLDIE
No that's what's fretting at me
I just fear
I was too hard on him
that's what it is

(Enter Gint.)

GINT
Good evening

OLDIE
God bless us it's my boy
how can that be
you still an outlaw

MAN
We won't say nothing

YOUNGER WOMAN
Not a word

OLDER WOMAN
We'll leave you alone now

OLDER MAN

(To Gint.)

See to yore mother
(Man, Older Woman, Older Man, Younger Woman leave and sit apart in dim light on the ramps, backs turned.)

GINT

I had to come see my Oldie Momma
whatever happens

OLDIE

And you did
now I can go in peace

GINT

What do you mean go
where you off to now

OLDIE

Pete
I'm tired I'm near the end

GINT

Don't tell me that
ain't one thing by God it's another
are yore hands and feet cold

OLDIE

They are

(Gint rubs her hands and feet.)

GINT

Here you be all right

OLDIE

Look Pete nothing left they took everything
even the storybooks we read
left me the house to die in
and that's all

GINT

Forget all that Oldie Momma
let's chat you and me
like old times
let go what went wrong

and what's hurt and sore
this bed
it's so short
why ain't this the bed I slept in as a boy

OLDIE
It is

GINT
Remember Momma you sat by me here
and tucked this coverlet over me
like I do for you now

OLDIE
Yes we played sleds
the way old country people
made them big and strong in the mountains
and rode them everywhere

GINT
With good horses and true
to pull them
you got to have that

OLDIE
You do of a sartin

GINT
With whip in hand
to make them horses mind
gee-up thar

OLDIE
I sat right up front here

GINT
Proud as you could be

OLDIE
Oh oh

GINT
What's the matter

OLDIE
It's my back
it hurts on these boards

GINT
Stretch a little
here I'll hold you
OLDIE
Pete I'm moving
I'm going somewhere
it's powerful strong inside me
GINT
We'll take a trip together
just like we used to
OLDIE
I don't feel right
GINT
I tell you the brand new Governor
in his mansion house
is giving a dinner party
lie back agin me
while I drive you there
OLDIE
Pete
go where
GINT
Where we're invited
you and me both
(Gint mimes driving her on a mountain sled.)
Gee-up Blackie
oh yes sir we've moving now
when Big John and Blackie commence to gallop
OLDIE
Pete wait
what's that noise
GINT
I hung sleigh bells on the sled
that's what they are
OLDIE
No it's a rumbling in a distance

something else
GINT
Thunder over a lake
Momma see we're going right by it
OLDIE
I'm scared son
what's that I hear
sighing so strange and wild
GINT
Pine trees Momma
talking to each other
just sit still
I see light
blazing light
OLDIE
What can it be
GINT
Why it is the mansion of the Governor
windows and doors all open
can't you hear the music playing inside
where people are dancing
OLDIE
Oh yes I think I do
GINT
Ah-ha on the doorstep
stands the Governor hisself
and Oldie Momma right beside him
stands nobody less
than Jesus Christ our Lord
waving to us like any plain mountain man
waving come on in
OLDIE
They want to see us
GINT
Greet us with honor Momma
handshakes friendship

some wine too I bet
OLDIE
Will Jesus give us cake with the wine
GINT
Of a sartin
reckon the Governor's wife
is getting you desert and coffee right now
whilst Jesus waves
OLDIE
I'm to meet important people
GINT
They'll come to meet us
like old friends and family
OLDIE
Oh Pete what a journey
GINT
Gee-up Blackie
Hey there Big John
OLDIE
Pete are we on the right road
GINT
Right down the big driveway Momma
OLDIE
The trip's a-tiring me out though son
GINT
There's the mansion rising up afore us
it'll soon be over
OLDIE
I'll lay back again you
my boy
I'll trust to you
GINT
Hold up now Big John Blackie too
Pete Gint and his mother have arrived
how do Governor
hidy Lord Jesus

shall we come in
you will look through these mountains
a long time
before you'll find a soul good as her
don't worry about me
we know what I am
but her pay her reverence give her respect
and tell her she's at home
and you Lord Jesus

(Oldie closes her eyes.)

we trust you will do the same
see Momma the Lord Jesus
Oldie Momma
say something
Momma
it's Pete yore son
Oh
you get to rest now
yore journey's over
I thank you for all the rides we took
thank you for the beatings
for the hugs and kisses too
now you must thank me as well
and pay yore driver
with a kiss

(Gint presses her lips to his cheek.)

there my Oldie Momma
that was my fare
all I charge
you're paid in full

(Enter Man, Older Man, Older Woman, And Younger Woman.)

YOUNGER WOMAN
Are you all right

GINT
Yes
since I can't do it myself
will you see my mother
buried with honor

OLDER MAN
We will

GINT
Give her quilt to Sally Vicks

OLDER WOMAN
We will

(Gint rocks his Oldie Momma gently back and forth.)

MAN
What will you do now

GINT
Go somewhere
make something of myself
like she wanted

OLDER WOMAN
Where

GINT
From the mountains to the sea

YOUNGER WOMAN
That far

GINT
And farther still

(Simple music. Light fades on Gint, his arms around Oldie Momma, rocking her back and forth.)

END OF ACT ONE

ACT TWO

All the actors come onto the platform again.

OLDER MAN
In Act Two, the six actors play six billionaires
YOUNGER WOMAN
A mistress
OLDER MAN
Six lunatics in an asylum
OLDER WOMAN
The Devil as a woman
OLDER MAN
A Preacher
MAN
A Mysterious Stranger
WOMAN
And Appalachian Brown Mountain Lights
(They make a line at the front of the platform.)
OLDER MAN
It is forty years later
OLDER WOMAN
The place is from California across the country to Appalachia again
YOUNGER WOMAN
Gint is now a white haired man of 75 in wonderful physical condition
MAN
Over the years
WOMAN
He becomes rich

YOUNGER MAN
He becomes *very rich*
ALL
We are the six billionaires
(*They sit on a circle, as if watching the sea at a resort.*)
Something must be done
(*Gint comes down between them at C. They are on the veranda of his luxury hotel.*)

GINT
Look my friends
how do you like my California view
the mountains the sea

WOMAN
So how did you do it
stay so young all these years

GINT
The first duty of the soldier
is to keep his body
in perfect condition
I do the same
while enjoying wine many women songs
and hotel verandas like this one
I trust you like it

OLDER WOMAN
California resort hotels
splendid view of your private airport
but let's talk money

OLDER MAN
Yes really money money
let's talk money

MAN
How much money
oh look there's the airplane
we flew in on
there on your private airstrip

OLDER MAN
Right on time

GINT
Yes that's my plane
but I didn't order it

OLDER WOMAN
Never mind who ordered it
at 75
you're not only younger than men half your age
you are much richer

WOMAN
Than anyone in fact except us

OLDER MAN
Do tell we must know

GINT
Well a poor boy came down from the mountains
searching for himself
and found himself

ALL
OH PLEASE

MAN
Come now stop that

WOMAN
You're among equals
down and dirty details please

OLDER WOMAN
After the first war twenties and thirties
we know about prohibition
the unions and the films guns and dope
but they don't add up to all you have

WOMAN
More than my tobacco or my gin

OLDER WOMAN
Or my cosmetics and medicine

OLDER MAN
We all made our millions
three wars didn't hurt

YOUNGER WOMAN
Since you initiated this meeting
flying us here in your own private planes
come clean

ALL
WHY ARE WE HERE

GINT
There's going to be another war

MAN
Where

GINT
Near China
where the French have lost everything
someone will have to step in
and that's why I brought you here

YOUNGER MAN .
Start a war

OLDER WOMAN
You want our money
to start a war

GINT
Never start anything like that
No I am a man of peace

OLDER MAN
But if there is war
supplies must be supplied

GINT
And that's a different matter

OLDER WOMAN
Your proposal

GINT
I need your resources as well as mine
to replace outworn countries
their governments outdated now
nationalism a thing of the past
we will be our own country our own nation

we will call ourselves Gintiana
you can call me
Emperor
MAN
Really
YOUNGER MAN
That's it then
OLDER WOMAN
We just give it to him
WOMAN
Here comes that plane
OLDER WOMAN
Taxiing up already
GINT
My airplane
OLDER MAN
So you think
GINT
But I didn't order one now
MAN
Gint did you think we would crown you
Emperor over ourselves
YOUNGER WOMAN
We have been watching you
long before this
MAN
You don't hustle people like us
no matter how much money you make
before we take action
OLDER WOMAN
With resources you cannot imagine
OLDER MAN
Your corporations have all been taken over
without your knowing it
the empire of Gint

liquidated as of today
everything that was yours
is ours

WOMAN
You don't even own this hotel now
or the airplane you sent
to bring us here we do

YOUNGER WOMAN
We left you your banks accounts
and a few Swiss stocks maybe

MAN
Get off this veranda
out of this hotel by tonight
it's ours too

(They exit off the platform and form a line at one side facing him.)

OLDER MAN
You had a good forty years

MAN
Now you're on your own again
we're off

WOMAN
Best of luck

ALL
BYE

(They stand there, close together. Gint stares out front, astounded.)

GINT
My God my God
this is a nightmare
they're in my own airplane
my pilot my steward serving them
traitors
they're taking off
I'm finished
I thought them weaker than I was
and they've closed the door on me
I've lost my power

oh God
make them come back
turn around and come back
it was all a joke
wasn't it
God where is your justice your wrath

ALL

B A N G

(A red light. Gint falls to the floor. Pause.)

B O O M

(Pause.)

ALL

AHHHHHHH

(They all scream, the screams then dying down into moans, whimpers, and silence.)

GINT

The airplane's blown up
they're all dead
God God I'm sorry
I didn't mean that
well yes maybe I did
I'm still alive
yes God

(Lights become normal.)

And I still have some money
I can still enjoy life
well women anyway
all right loving
I'll live for that

(Younger Woman moves to Gint. He puts his arm around her in a fatherly way, and they walk together to one of the ramps.)

Young women make this mistake
they think what a man looks like
is what he is
I'm just plain down to earth me
ordinary looking fellow
myself and nothing but myself
here let's sit under this mulberrry tree

so we can get to know each other
YOUNGER WOMAN
I think you're a wonderful man
and I want to learn wonderful things from you
(Gint lies on a ramp. Younger Woman sits beside him.)
GINT
I'll teach you what's important
and what's not
never mind what most people say
how to stay young that's the secret
old birds lose their feathers
old women their teeth
and old men you know what well
what's intelligence what's smart
come a little closer
and I'll show you
good now I'm going to give you
everything you want money jewels
but most of all me
just climb up on top there that's it
(The Younger Woman sits on Gint, her skirt around him. They begin to have sex.)
YOUNGER WOMAN
This what you mean
GINT
Exactly and you'll find that soon
you'll be mine alone
you'll belong to me
just me and nothing else but me
(Gint begins to breathe with difficulty.)
YOUNGER WOMAN
You all right Poppa
GINT
Never better
I'm only seventy-five
I'll live forever

YOUNGER WOMAN
Happy now are you honey
GINT
Absolutely
only when the juices
are flowing can a man be himself
and nothing but himself
YOUNGER WOMAN
Ummm yes Poppa
GINT
Whooopeee
YOUNGER WOMAN
You give me cash I keep us going
now that's the way it works
GINT
Everything
I'll sign it all away
it's all yours
hell why not
I'm still feisty
what else is there

(Younger Woman stares at Gint as he has increasing difficulty. Finally, he gives up, and his arms fall away from her. He lies impotent under her.)

YOUNGER WOMAN
You're older than you think Poppa
what was there is gone

(She gets up, touches him not unkindly but business like on the cheek.)

thanks Poppa
you were good for your age
so long

(Exit Younger Woman. Gint sits up, laughs.)

GINT
Gone my fortune
gone my dreams of Gintiana
now wine woman song gone

I've lost my sex
gone yonder too

(A long pause.)

yonder
I said yonder
sound like a hick again
haven't talked like that in a half a century
well I'm still man enough
to seek things philosophical
befitting my age
and experience
let me consider
time and the ages
take refuge in the sure harbors
of the mind
if I can't be Emperor of the World
I will rule the Intellect
survey all that history unfolds
and from the study of kingdoms their
rise and fall learn the inner secrets
of mortal wisdom yes that's it
with my brain and nothing but my brain
let me analyze deeds worthy
of good old Pete Gint
his weapon his brain and nothing but his brain
so where to study

(Enter Older Man.)

OLDER MAN
You

GINT
Huh

OLDER MAN
What's your name

GINT
Pete Gint that's me

OLDER MAN
I have found you

                at last
              come with me
                 GINT
                 Where

               OLDER MAN
             To your subjects
             who wait for you
        follow you and understand you
                 GINT
        People still think about me someplace
               OLDER MAN
          You wanted to be an Emperor
              I'll show you where
       you are Emperor of all the Emperors
                who ever lived
                 GINT
              You can where

               OLDER MAN
             At my Establishment
           with people who know you
               come come come

(The Older Man takes Gint off, down a ramp. Up another ramp come Older Woman, Woman, Man, Younger Man, and Younger Man. They are very bright eyed and eager. They place the large box at C. Enter Older Man and Gint, to a ramp, facing the platform.)

                 GINT
           This is a strange building
              nobody at the gates
                or the office
               OLDER MAN
      It is undergoing a change of administration
             my friends you see here
            they are the interpreters
                 GINT
             Interpreters of what

OLDER MAN
For one thing
Huhu

GINT
What

(Man, Woman, Younger Woman, Older Woman sit on the box.)

OLDER MAN
One of our greatest accomplishments
published all over the world
its creator here before you

(Younger Man addresses them with logic and conviction.)

YOUNGER MAN
My name is John Huhu
inventor of Huhu
I took apart
the language of apes
and found in it the hidden specifics
of original communication
creating Huhu I made sense
of previously threadbare intellectual concepts
and exploded all other assumptions about everything
now since previous human language
especially Linear B Greek
Latin French, German and English
is gibberish
only my ape language named Huhu for me
describes anything correctly
therefore I and my colleagues are sole interpreters
of reality deconstructed through Huhu
we are the only human beings
who can explain anything to you
in Huhu

(All applaud. Younger Man joins them.)

GINT
Very interesting

OLDER MAN
You see the range of our research here

this is truly a great university
(Woman stands on the box, equally impassioned.)

WOMAN
My name is Doctor Thigh
Using my theory of
Psychicphysicalizationismstrasse
I identified the inverse outverse
co-opted sexual domination
of recurring language in Supreme Court decisions
as actually screened masturbation fantasies encoded
by Pentagon Generals for purposes of sexual research
I recognized this monumental truth
waking one morning
my theory of psychicphysicalizationismstrasse
in my brain right between my eyes
while my right hand
found its way right between my legs
and bang I knew the Truth

GINT
I'm getting out of here
(He tries to run away. They all grab him.)

ALL
No no no no
(They stop Gint, turn the box on end and sit him on it.)

OLDER MAN
No you belong here
many are the marvels we have accomplished
but the greatest happened today
when at eleven o'clock precisely
Reason died

GINT
Reason what

OLDER MAN
Absolute reason rule of the world
dead sir at eleven o'clock
gentlemen ladies all hail
Emperor of All Thought

Pete Gint

ALL

Hooray Pete Gint
Hooray Pete Gint
Hooray Pete Gint

GINT

Where am I

OLDER MAN

You are at Great University Hospital
which today claimed its
truthful name Great University

GINT

This is what happened at eleven o'clock

YOUNGER MAN AND YOUNGER WOMAN

(In unison.)

We took over

OLDER MAN

The previous administration
proven incompetent was replaced by its staff
us

MAN

As all intellectual establishments
are replaced
done away with

GINT

Killed
staff means inmates
lunatics
you killed your keepers

MAN

Lunatic is a very imprecise word
in a modern university
exactly who is mentally what
in a place like this
is often a matter of considerable
conjecture and publication in obscure journals

OLDER WOMAN
Anyway we run this place now
with you our Emperor
GINT
Really can't sorry good-bye
I have to save myself
(All groan, keep Gint up on the box.)
ALL
No no no
WOMAN
Don't you see
it is here
in the Empire of Thought
we most save ourselves
and nothing else at all
(The Older Woman stands next to Gint. She is in a rapture.)
OLDER WOMAN
Each of us shuts ourselves up
in a barrel of self
in our own fermentation we dive to the bottom
of all our lives
sealed hermetically with the resin of thought
we live ambered through seasons of self
no tears for anybody else's troubles
no thoughts for anybody else's ideas
all we need is an Emperor to represent us
and everyone knows you are the man
(The Younger Man steps forward. He holds his finger in the air.)
YOUNGER MAN
I do have a problem
You see this electric screwdriver
ALL
Hmmmmmmmmmmmmmmmm
YOUNGER MAN
well my computer brain
after all my labors
deprogrammed itself

I can no longer compute the Huhu
I have to write
I need you to fix me
with this
just stick it inside my head
GINT
Be careful with that thing
its whirring you turned it on
YOUNGER MAN
In my eye do you think
or my mouth
you do it
GINT
Wait turn it off
I can't help you
YOUNGER MAN
But you must
if I can't write jargon
no one will know what I'm good for
education politics business
I'll be out of date fix me
OLDER MAN
Emperor your first command
GINT
First command
computer heal thyself
how's that
OLDER MAN
You heard him
The Emperor
YOUNGER MAN
Wise Emperor I salute you
I will heal my brain at once
oh sweet electricity
deliver me

ALL
BUZZZZZZZZZZZZZ

GINT
Wait I didn't mean that
turn that thing off

YOUNGER MAN
Rapture ecstasy
to electrify my brains
puddle them into blood
my mind my mind

GINT
Stop

(The Younger Man mimes plunging the electric drill into his ear and goes behind the box.)

ALL
BUZZZZZZZZZZZZZZZZZZZZZZZZZ

GINT
Wait stop that man
Christ he's drilling out his brains

ALL
LONG LIVE THE EMPEROR
THE EMPEROR OF SELF

(Gint jumps off the box, over the lunatics and runs away. The box is set slanting on the platform, and becomes the back end of a truck. Gint and the Older Woman sit on it, traveling.)

GINT
I tell you it was a nuthouse
and I got out of there fast

OLDER WOMAN
Quite a life you've had
where are you now

GINT
Well I lost my money
then love making
then philosophy and
decided I'd seek wisdom on the road

in travel
OLDER WOMAN
Like me
GINT
Yes I took off across the country
hitching rides in old trucks like this one
crossed the Rockies
over the Mississippi
down to the Gulf of Mexico
fished in Everglade City
drank in Key West
until my liver gave out
then years went by
one thing and another
brought me back where I am now
here
all I know
OLDER WOMAN
In other words
you don't know what you're doing
or where you're going
do you
GINT
I am just me
myself and nothing but myself
way I been all my born days
OLDER WOMAN
Born days bet you haven't said that
in years neither

(She points.)

There's the Blue Ridge escarpment
we are near Qualla Cherokee Land
steep meadows and balds in timothy grass
dark lakes and pines
like where you were born
GINT
How do you know where I was born

OLDER WOMAN
Just do
why I recall when it was
all lonely up here
first horses and sleds then wagons
then tiny T model Fords crawling up windy roads
now you got cars like space ships
all the same to me
I just live on the road
meeting people like you

GINT
But you're a woman how can you
live on the road it's dangerous

OLDER WOMAN
Oh men seem to leave me alone
just something about me
(She drapes a leg over one of Gint's legs.)
you want a piece of me Gint
(They both laugh.)

GINT
God no begging your pardon
I'd just rather not

OLDER WOMAN
How old do you think you are

GINT
Not exactly sure
head's a little cloudy just haven't kept up
way into my eighties anyhow

OLDER WOMAN
You are ninety five

GINT
I'm what how do you know that

OLDER WOMAN
Just do and never been married am I right

GINT
Never and glad of it

(They laugh.)

OLDER WOMAN
Look at all them houses
families at home
little children too
what do you think of that

GINT
Waiting for Daddy
home he comes
Swears at them

OLDER WOMAN
I'll not have this

GINT
God damn that

OLDER WOMAN
Little tykes scared wide-eyed
wives screaming knocked down
run to Grandma's house

GINT
She's just as mean as he was

OLDER WOMAN
Leaving the son of a bitch

GINT
For the mother

GINT AND OLDER WOMAN
Of the son of a bitch

GINT
Then slinking back home

OLDER WOMAN
Then all over again

GINT
Family life

OLDER WOMAN
You want no part of it right

GINT
No but
(Gint stops laughing. So does she.)
OLDER WOMAN
But what
GINT
To have somebody waiting
somewhere
would be right nice
right nice
haven't talked like that in years
(Older Woman grabs Gint's hand, presses it to her body ferociously.)
OLDER WOMAN
Feel me up Gint
feel these nipples still hard and juicy
this belly still strong
this twitchet still twitching
and here down to my knee
down to my ankle
now
what's this
GINT
My God it's a hoof
OLDER WOMAN
Right
GINT
You the devil
OLDER WOMAN
A piece of him
GINT
That's how you knowed
so much about me
OLDER WOMAN
Knowed you said knowed
well I've knowed you all your life

oh yes you've been the Devil's own
and you'd be damned right now
but you are on your way to another country
where you are none of mine
I'm hopping off now
so long Gint

GINT
What do you mean another country
(Older Woman jumps off the box.)

OLDER WOMAN
You'll see
have fun being old
(Exit Older Woman. Gint gets of the box.)

GINT
Crazy old woman
not no devil
but this truck is slowing down
I best stop thinking so much
hop off
(Gint does, looks around.)
Some kind of cemetery uh-ho
(Gint moves back. The six actors take the oblong box, and carrying it as a coffin, set it down at center. They gather beside it, as at a grave.)

A funeral
Thank God it ain't ISN'T mine
(The Older Man, as an explosive mountain preacher, preaches with quiet then rising passion to them over the coffin.)

OLDER MAN
He come to Cave Cove at war time
our soldiers went proudly to death World War I
him standing before the army
showing sergeants a right arm one hand gone
him two handed
three days before
he never denied what he done

GINT
At's him I saw him cut that hand off
over fifty years ago
OLDER MAN
He went to live hard above the waterfalls
found a wife who took him
children soon
and to them he was not a disgrace
coming to town with that stump arm
getting his week's supply of our scorn
along with his bread
(He gets evangelistic and emotional.)
flood washed him out
never a word of complaint
fire burned down his cabin
he rebuilt that
with that stump arm
and prospered again
the worst winter we ever knowed
blasted his crops killed his wife nearly
finished him but onct again
the tiny farm gave forth its life
to a one-handed draft dodger
(He quiets down.)
then his children grown up and handsome
went off and forgot him
having learned
to be ashamed of their father
and he lived alone with his disgrace
through other days
and other wars
(Emotional again.)
Oh my God
modern wars
men come back crazy from that war
they took drugs to ease
memories of women and children slaughtered
what they had done to others

and suffered themselves for their country
and still can't forget
while he who cut off his hand
farmed forgotten
until this morning when he died

GINT
At's him then

OLDER MAN

(Quiets down again.)

So we have come together to bury this man
he was no neighbor
he was no patriot
he grew nothing for state or church
but there on land almost upside down
he made up his mind who he was
he saw his humble calling in his life
and there he quietly lived
because he was himself
because he paid his price openly before us
his silence in war rang true

(He suddenly preaches hell fire.)

before he'd kill a man with that right hand
he cut it off
like the Bible says
if thy right hand offend thee
like the Bible says
cut it off and he did it
he didn't just say it
oh no my God he did it
praise God

ALL
Praise God

OLDER MAN

Therefore whatever we may think
of his duty in that time of war
let peace be with him now
it is not for us to judge the heart

or the dust to which it falls
that is for heaven
but let me dare to speak for him here
I hope this man self crippled in our life
stands whole and true before God
Amen

ALL
Amen

(They all pick up the coffin and take it away.)

GINT
So that's what become of him
well it don't have nothing to do with me
old Pete Gint
he is what he is
poor but honest
himself and nothing but himself
let's see now
what if I go northeast from here

(Enter Man.)

MAN
Old man

GINT
Yes

MAN
You know an old geezer named Gint

GINT
If it's Pete Gint here he stands

MAN
Lucky me
you're the man

GINT
I'm the man what

MAN
I was sent after today

GINT
The hell are you talking about

what do you want
MAN
You
for my sack
GINT
Poke that's what I called a sack
when I was a boy
why do I keep doing this
talking like I talked then
what about your poke
MAN
You're going in it
GINT
Git out of here
MAN
In these mountains today
you'll cross a dozen highways
with signs stores tourist rides
golf courses and ski slopes
filthy smoke out of cars and trucks
choking you half to death
before you get there right
GINT
Modern life the way it is now so
MAN
So I know a man
who raises chickens
GINT
Chickens
MAN
For all those eggs
thousands of chickens
just one problem
those chickens roost in mile long sheds
drop mile long shit into mile long metal pans
somebody has to clean it mile long well

my smart chicken farmer invented
a kind of foam
you spray it on those pans all that chickenshit
sticks to it
makes a blanket of foam
you just pull up throw it away
and everything in it
peels away mile long metal pans
all shiny and clean again

GINT

What does chickenshit have to do with me
I'm getting out of here
(The Medicine Man closes his eyes and spreads his arms wide.)

MAN

The Spirit That Measures All Things
will in the second dawn of time
pull away all you have shit on the earth
it will all just lift up and be thrown to darkness
and under that as it was in Cherokee time
will be the meadows and the animals
flowers plants deer bear fish
earth fire water and air
we will live again
as once my nation did
when our life was sacred
when we killed for food
but blessed worshipped and became
the animals we killed

GINT

You're a God damned Cherokee Indian

MAN

I'm a God damned Cherokee Medicine Man
living with truth you cannot imagine

GINT

Oh yes like what

MAN

Your worthless self goes in my poke

and then to a fire burning you up
good souls can go back in the earth
into trees brush plants loam
that is honorable death
yours is to become nothing
but chickenshit and dirty air
and then you vanish

GINT

And who gives you the right to do this to me

MAN

Again you will not understand
The Spirit That Measures All Things

GINT

I understand all right
you don't have a pot to piss in
look at your boots ten years old if a day
raggedy ass clothes falling off you
hell all you Indians were killing each other
when we came
wartime all the time
paint your nose kill your neighbor
until we finally put you in your place
now here you are
telling me about spirits that rule us all
while you live in a tar paper shack somewhere

MAN

A tar paper shack so rooted in life
it will stand
when skyscrapers fall
that is home
something you don't have at all
home what was that
you never knew
you weren't good or bad
you took everything so lightly
nothing stuck
a splash of mud maybe you are

a mess but a mess with a soul
which goes now into my black poke

GINT

Oh stop it
I am myself
if anybody ever was

MAN

And what was that nothing
had you lived otherwise
giving something of yourself
no matter how crazy you were
if you thought once of someone else
it might be different

GINT

I'll play along
beat you at your own game
just give me a little time
I'll prove I was myself
honest and true
and made something of myself
like I was supposed to

MAN

How prove it

GINT

Witnesses I'll find them
how much time can I have

MAN

You are a fiesty old man
I'll give you that
all right one day
until darkness falls

GINT

Done

MAN

Until the dusk Gint

(Man turns his back. Change of light.)

GINT
I got to go fast now
find me a witness
(Enter Older Man. He is in bad shape.)
OLDER MAN
Hey there buddy
how about a dollar for an old man
down and out
GINT
Here's a dollar keep it
OLDER MAN
Why hell it's Pete Gint
GINT
Do I know you
OLDER MAN
You was almost my God damned son in law buddy
don't you remember me
GINT
You
OLDER MAN
I have come down a tad in the world
my mountain sold for tourists
they walk through my caverns now
eating popcorn
but it's me
GINT
Best witness I could find
OLDER MAN
Witness to what
GINT
What I did what I was
OLDER MAN
Oh yeah well you were smart
not marrying that daughter of mine
turned out bad lived in Memphis

left her kid one man after anothern
yore brat growed up crazy as you are

GINT
I need a witness
I'll give you another dollar
two maybe three

OLDER MAN
For what

GINT
You wanted to scratch my eyeball remember
make a razorback hog out of me
I refused
stood on my own two feet and said no

OLDER MAN
But when you left us
you took it with you
the razorback hog of us
its motto branded on you
the motto that separates hogs from men

GINT
What damn hog motto

OLDER MAN
I will be myself
and nothing but myself

GINT
And nothing but myself
I got that from you

OLDER MAN
Nowhere else
you lived a razorback hog ever since
you did it brother and how
the greatest hog of all time

GINT
Damn you're no witness

OLDER MAN
Too bad see you

(Exit Older Man. It is getting darker.)

      GINT
     What's this
      mist
   sliding down in this gorge
   can't see a damn thing
     oh lights

(Enter Younger Man, Woman, Older Woman, Younger Woman, who all face Gint.)

    pale mountain lights
    phosphorous rising up
     spirits Cherokees say
maybe there's something to that Medicine Man

     OLDER WOMAN
     Pete Gint

     YOUNGER MAN
    You betrayed us

     OLDER WOMAN
     You left us

    YOUNGER WOMAN
   Thoughts and songs

     YOUNGER MAN
    Tears and deeds

     OLDER WOMAN
    Races and truths

     YOUNGER MAN
    We are thoughts

    YOUNGER WOMAN
   You should have thought

     OLDER WOMAN
     And did not

     YOUNGER MAN
     We are tears

     OLDER WOMAN
   You should have shed

YOUNGER WOMAN
And did not
YOUNGER MAN
Races never run
deeds never done
YOUNGER MAN
We are the truths
YOUNGER WOMAN
You should have told
WOMAN
And did not
GINT
Stop it
I did my best
I was myself
be witnesses to it
(Gint reaches out to them. They push him away roughly and leave.)
ALL
(Overlapping.)

Look at us now
shrunken and wasted
unused and deformed
you slept our life away
going around
being yourself
not good not bad
nothing
you killed us
it's too late now
good-bye good-bye good-bye
(They exit. Light changes. Gint sits up.)
GINT
My conscience gone
now what
oh God dusk

(Man turns around.)

MAN
Well witnesses
GINT
None you were right
But then what did it mean
be myself and nothing but myself
MAN
Here catch
(Man tosses Gint an imaginary onion.)
GINT
What's this
looks like a good old Vidalia onion
I loved as a boy
layers and layers around a juicy heart
MAN
Then peel yourself
(Gint peels off layers of onion skin.)
GINT
All right
to the heart
away with the outside
off with the runaway
the gentleman living in luxury
good-bye millionaire
pleasure of the flesh forget it
this looks like a crown forget that
down with the nuthouse
so long all my travels
good-bye all my
can't hold this one oh that's enough
let's get to the juicy heart of Gint
right here
nothing
it was all just layers
at the center of me
my self gone

MAN
In the sack
let's go

GINT
I misremember everthang now
who I am what I am why I am
my life is like that loony house I was in
my age befuddles me badly
am I alive what happened to me
ain't hardly mannerable to talk to
getting less and leaster ever minute
I don't begrudge you no powers now
only let me climb that there hill
see one more dawn breaking
see the sun come up one last time
cuss you out
then give it up
and go in yore poke
how's that

MAN
Too bad you didn't amount to something Gint
you might have made a passable Cherokee
instead of a miserable white man
I'll give you 'til sun up then
(Exit Man. Gint goes to the bottom of one of the ramps, turns and begins to climb slowly to the top of the platform.)

GINT
Jest a trace of nothing
a gray vanishment in the mist
all I was
(All hum music played at the beginning of the play.)
oh heavenlike day
yore goodness is all frittered in my empty soul
not a living creature here to come get warm
at the touch of yore sun ball hand
but I was fixing to climb
however foolish
so I'll climb this here last little hill

straight on this time
no Bresh what I done all my life
not round about
not this time
I'll climb straight on
after that
let be what will

(As he climbs, Sally Vicks climbs also, bringing the small crate to the C. of the platform and sits on it, looking around. She puts the quilt over her legs. Humming stops.)

SALLY VICKS
Can't hardly see but it's you
ain't it

GINT
Sally Vicks
still alive

SALLY VICKS
Why not you are

GINT
They say I'm a hundred

SALLY VICKS
Pert near me too

GINT
What are you doing here

SALLY VICKS
From here you left me
to this place I come
once ever day of my life

GINT
What for

SALLY VICKS
Looking for you
what else

GINT
Do tell

(Gint sits on the ground beside her.)

but all these years
you shorely didn't jest
sit on that crate
waiting fer me
SALLY VICKS
No I lived

GINT
Marry

SALLY VICKS
Two husbands
decent men I treasured
lived with in contentment
but they were not you

GINT
Chilluns grandchilluns

SALLY VICKS
Great grandchilluns
come to see me
when they can
dear to me as life can be
but they are not you

GINT
Then you kept a hold of me

SALLY VICKS
And never let go no sir

GINT
Then tell it to me
where was I
all this time

SALLY VICKS
you was here
in my faith
in my hope
in my love

GINT
It was you

I was a-coming back to
SALLY VICKS
I reckon
GINT
It was you
I was re-learning how to talk to
SALLY VICKS
That's possible
GINT
Can you for what little is left
abide me a-tall
SALLY VICKS
As easy as the flowers are made
can I abide you Pete
long as you want
GINT
Take me and keep me
SALLY VICKS
Of a sartin
rest your old body
twixt my old legs

(Gint lies sits down, resting his back against Sally Vicks, who spreads her legs for him. She spreads the quilt over them both.)

I'll be midwife momma and lover
at onct Pete Gint
GINT
Midwife momma lover
SALLY VICKS
Sleep
I cradle the baby
sleep
I comfort the boy
sleep
I love the man

(The Man appears behind them.)

MAN
The day will not last long
Pete Gint
then we will see
what you're made of
something or nothing

SALLY VICKS
I will watch over you
I will watch over you

(Simple music. Light fades on Pete Gint sleeping, and on Sally Vicks and the Man, both watching over him.)

END OF PLAY

PROPERTY LIST
Two sturdy crates
Quilt

WOOD WALL

RAMP

RAMP | PLATFORM 2' HIGH | RAMP

RAMP

CRATE

CRATE

QUILT

SCENE DESIGN "GINT"

(DESIGNED BY ROMULUS LINNEY AND MARK MERCANTE FOR THEATER FOR THE NEW CITY)

ST. MARY'S COLLEGE OF MARYLAND

3 3127 00187 7119

**PS 3562 .I55 G56 1999
Linney, Romulus, 1930-
Gint**

NEW PLAYS

- **SMASH by Jeffrey Hatcher.** Based on the novel, AN UNSOCIAL SOCIALIST by George Bernard Shaw, the story centers on a millionaire Socialist who leaves his bride on their wedding day because he fears his passion for her will get in the way of his plans to overthrow the British government. *"SMASH is witty, cunning, intelligent, and skillful."* –Seattle Weekly. *"SMASH is a wonderfully high-style British comedy of manners that evokes the world of Shaw's high-minded heroes and heroines, but shaped by a post modern sensibility."* –Seattle Herald. [5M, 5W] ISBN: 0-8222-1553-5

- **PRIVATE EYES by Steven Dietz.** A comedy of suspicion in which nothing is ever quite what it seems. *"Steven Dietz's ... Pirandellian smooch to the mercurial nature of theatrical illusion and romantic truth, Dietz's spiraling structure and breathless pacing provide enough of an oxygen rush to revive any moribund audience member ... Dietz's mastery of playmaking ... is cause for kudos."* –The Village Voice. *"The cleverest and most artful piece presented at the 21st annual [Humana] festival was PRIVATE EYES by writer-director Steven Dietz."* –The Chicago Tribune. [3M, 2W] ISBN: 0-8222-1619-1

- **DIMLY PERCEIVED THREATS TO THE SYSTEM by Jon Klein.** Reality and fantasy overlap with hilarious results as this unforgettable family attempts to survive the nineties. *"Here's a play whose point about fractured families goes to the heart, mind -- and ears."* –The Washington Post. *" ... an end-of-the millennium comedy about a family on the verge of a nervous breakdown ... Trenchant and hilarious ... "* –The Baltimore Sun. [2M, 4W] ISBN: 0-8222-1677-9

- **HONOUR by Joanna Murray-Smith.** In a series of intense confrontations, a wife, husband, lover and daughter negotiate the forces of passion, lust, history, responsibility and honour. *"Tight, crackling dialogue (usually played out in punchy verbal duels) captures characters unable to deal with emotions ... Murray-Smith effectively places her characters in situations that strip away pretense."* –Variety. *"HONOUR might just capture a few honors of its own."* –Time Out Magazine. [1M, 3W] ISBN: 0-8222-1683-3

- **NINE ARMENIANS by Leslie Ayvazian.** A revealing portrait of three generations of an Armenian-American family. *" ... Ayvazian's obvious personal exploration ... is evocative, and her picture of an American Life colored nostalgically by an increasingly alien ethnic tradition, is persuasively embedded into a script of a certain supple grace ... "* –The NY Post. *"... NINE ARMENIANS is a warm, likable work that benefits from ... Ayvazian's clear-headed insight into the dynamics of a close-knit family ... "* –Variety. [5M, 5W] ISBN: 0-8222-1602-7

- **PSYCHOPATHIA SEXUALIS by John Patrick Shanley.** Fetishes and psychiatry abound in this scathing comedy about a man and his father's argyle socks. *"John Patrick Shanley's new play, PSYCHOPATHIA SEXUALIS is ... perfectly poised between daffy comedy and believable human neurosis which Shanley combines so well ... "* –The LA Times. *"John Patrick Shanley's PSYCHOPATHIA SEXUALIS is a salty boulevard comedy with a bittersweet theme ... "* –New York Magazine. *"A tour de force of witty, barbed dialogue."* –Variety. [3M, 2W] ISBN: 0-8222-1615-9

DRAMATISTS PLAY SERVICE, INC.
440 Park Avenue South, New York, NY 10016 212-683-8960 Fax 212-213-1539
postmaster@dramatists.com www.dramatists.com

NEW PLAYS

- **A QUESTION OF MERCY by David Rabe.** The Obie Award-winning playwright probes the sensitive and controversial issue of doctor-assisted suicide in the age of AIDS in this poignant drama. *"There are many devastating ironies in Mr. Rabe's beautifully considered, piercingly clear-eyed work ... " –The NY Times. "With unsettling candor and disturbing insight, the play arouses pity and understanding of a troubling subject ... Rabe's provocative tale is an affirmation of dignity that rings clear and true." –Variety.* [6M, 1W] ISBN: 0-8222-1643-4

- **A DOLL'S HOUSE by Henrik Ibsen, adapted by Frank McGuinness. Winner of the 1997 Tony Award for best revival.** *"New, raw, gut-twisting and gripping. Easily the hottest drama this season." –USA Today. "Bold, brilliant and alive." –The Wall Street Journal. "A thunderclap of an evening that takes your breath away." –Time. "The stuff of Broadway legend." –Associated Press.* [4M, 4W, 2 boys] ISBN: 0-8222-1636-1

- **THE WAITING ROOM by Lisa Loomer.** Three women from different centuries meet in a doctor's waiting room in this dark comedy about the timeless quest for beauty -- and its cost. *" ... THE WAITING ROOM ... is a bold, risky melange of conflicting elements that is ... terrifically moving ... There's no resisting the fierce emotional pull of the play." –The NY Times. " ... one of the high points of this year's Off-Broadway season ... THE WAITING ROOM is well worth a visit." –Back Stage.* [7M, 4W, flexible casting] ISBN: 0-8222-1594-2

- **MR. PETERS' CONNECTIONS by Arthur Miller.** Mr. Miller describes the protagonist as existing in a dream-like state when the mind is "freed to roam from real memories to conjectures, from trivialities to tragic insights, from terror of death to glorying in one's being alive." With this memory play, the Tony Award and Pulitzer Prize-winner reaffirms his stature as the world's foremost dramatist. *" ... a cross between Joycean stream-of-consciousness and Strindberg's dream plays, sweetened with a dose of William Saroyan's philosophical whimsy ... CONNECTIONS is most intriguing ... Miller scholars will surely find many connections of their own to make between this work and the author's earlier plays." –The NY Times.* [5M, 3W] ISBN: 0-8222-1687-6

- **THE STEWARD OF CHRISTENDOM by Sebastian Barry.** A freely imagined portrait of the author's great-grandfather, the last Chief Superintendent of the Dublin Metropolitan Police. *"MAGNIFICENT ... the cool, elegiac eye of James Joyce's THE DEAD; the bleak absurdity of Samuel Beckett's lost, primal characters; the cosmic anger of KING LEAR ..." –The NY Times. "Sebastian Barry's compassionate imaging of an ancestor he never knew is among the most poignant onstage displays of humanity in recent memory." –Variety.* [5M, 4W] ISBN: 0-8222-1609-4

- **SYMPATHETIC MAGIC by Lanford Wilson. Winner of the 1997 Obie for best play.** The mysteries of the universe, and of human and artistic creation, are explored in this award-winning play. *"Lanford Wilson's idiosyncratic SYMPATHETIC MAGIC is his BEST PLAY YET ... the rare play you WANT ... chock-full of ideas, incidents, witty or poetic lines, scientific and philosophical argument ... you'll find your intellectual faculties racing." –New York Magazine. "The script is like a fully notated score, next to which most new plays are cursory lead sheets." –The Village Voice.* [5M, 3W] ISBN: 0-8222-1630-2

DRAMATISTS PLAY SERVICE, INC.
440 Park Avenue South, New York, NY 10016 212-683-8960 Fax 212-213-1539
postmaster@dramatists.com www.dramatists.com